Pain on the Edge

Alexandra Dolgov

Presentation by *BookLeaf Publishing*

Web: www.bookleafpub.com

E-mail: info@bookleafpub.com

ISBN: 9789357441476

First edition 2023

DEDICATION

I dedicate this book to myself and you. This is our book, our love, and our pain.

I deserve this - you know how bad I wanted this. I hope you love it and please don't feel bad for me, and please don't take the words too close to heart cause all these feelings are passing by but my love for you will never die.

ACKNOWLEDGEMENT

I do not want to sound like Snoop Dogg, but I want to thank myself for allowing me to love and let this pain become a book. I want to thank Victor because I know he will be the first supporter when he gets to see this book being real, even if it's only poems, and we have talked so many times about me putting a book into the real world. For his support and the nights he spend in the garden with me while I was crying and just talking about everything.

I want to thank P. for being the man he is and for everything we have been through together. I love you and I will never stop loving you for being you. Our love didn't make it, but what I learned about loving you changed my life and it changed me as well.

With you, I understood that I am not what happened to me, I am what I built for myself, even if I don't have anybody, even if I am not happy at all. It's my responsibility to live and nobody else's.

PREFACE

The stages of a breakup mostly have been forever structured as grief stages of denial, anger, bargaining, depression, and acceptance. We don't know which ones are the most unbearable to experience, but I know the one that everyone is healing toward to - acceptance.

Last year was the most painful in my life, but I am still healing and learning. So read this book and look into my stories of love, pain, and forgiveness. And please know that love is greater than pain and tears because love should always be unconditional. And please remember the words of the great Maya Angelou, 'Have enough courage to trust love one more time and always one more time.'

I wish I wasn't that kind of woman...

...where she gets crazy about one man who doesn't want her or doesn't have the time for her.

I wish I wasn't that kind of woman who will always let that man in again, and again and again; cause she always remembers that love needs one more chance every day.

I wish I wasn't that kind of woman who will fall for passionate kisses and hot nights in bed.

I wish I wasn't that kind of woman who tries to protect herself from lies and 'empty' promises.

I wish I wasn't that kind of woman who tries to fix other mistakes when she wasn't at fault.

I wish I wasn't that kind of woman who can't let go easily. Who keeps dreaming and texting late at night and keeps that door open?

I wish to be more of a woman focusing on her career. I wish to be more of a woman who doesn't need love to go on. I wish to be more of

a woman who doesn't belong to any city, man,
or universe.

I wish to be that kind of woman who doesn't
have all this passion in her.

Dreaming of nightmares

I fell in love with the man of my dreams,
While I was being his nightmare.

He broke my heart like a mirror,
And I still looked through the piece and stayed for
love.

I blamed myself to love too much, too passionately,
too fiercely,
Because you wanted me quiet and drown my fire.

I have fallen in love with my man of dreams,
But I have forgotten myself while dreaming.

I ignored the flags, I endorse them one by one,
Because of the love I never tasted,
Because of the fire, I kept alive,
Because of the little girl's hope inside me,
Because of love that never stopped.

And then I kept choosing my dream man,
While the woman became his nightmare.

Mad

Mad that you are happy
Mad I have lost so much
And you move on like nothing.

Tears rolling and screaming
And still, you didn't hear my heart.

Mad that your love never existed
Mad I let you in and signed the docs,
And you still didn't fake your try with me.

My heart ripped out of my chest
And still, you didn't let that bother you.

Mad that I made myself for you,
Mad I let you break and dust
And you just roll over me.

Crushing my soul into the ground
And still, it didn't hurt you at all.

Daily failures of an open heart

You knew I wasn't your woman
And still, you made me yours
You knew the kind of love I was seeking
And still, you didn't even try
You knew my flaws and my hopes
and still, you didn't call it quits
You knew my tears and my dreams
and still, you didn't move.

I tried to be your woman
I tried to marry you
I tried to keep my silence
I tried to keep my tears
I tried again and again through infidelity
And still, you didn't change.

My only fault was that I believed in you
Being my soulmate more than I was to myself.
Your fault was stopping me from leaving
With I love yous and I am yours.

Imagine

I imagine myself leaving, putting my stuff in the car,
Looking behind me as I tried to move the boxes,
And I wish I never left you behind.

I wish I never asked you to love me
I wish I had never broken a man that can't love me
I wish I never cried and chase you
I wish I was the woman I kept showing you - the mad
one, the I don't care one, the go-to-hell one.

I imagine me crying at your chest, asking how am I
gonna live now without you,
And I wished I never pushed you to do anything you
don't want.
I wish I never asked for flowers and candlelight
dinners,
I wish I never accepted you from the start
I wish I never said I am happy
I wish I never let you in my life.

I imagine me screaming and crying on the phone with
you while I drive,
And I wished I didn't feel the betrayal the day before.
I wish I was never sick and you weren't disgusted
I wish I was the quiet and calm woman
I wish I never send the long texts and explanation
I wish so many things didn't ever happen.

But all this was not my imagination
All these situations were real and I felt them.
And it was not my imagination that I still didn't
get to feel your love in my kind of way.

Silence

I will never forgive you
For the silence
While I was pacing like a caged animal.

I will never forgive you
For the silence
While I was crying with no air to take.

I will never forgive you
For the silence
While I was wearing my tongue and heart on my
sleeve.

I will never forgive you
For the silence
While I was fighting to get you back again and
again.

I will never forgive you
For the silence
While I was on the edge of my pain.

I will never forgive you
For the silence
Because it was so loud I couldn't stand.

What we made out of love...

Its past 1 AM and I can't shut up my brain
My face is swollen and my jaw is hurting crying,
And all I think about is how good will it be
again
To kiss you and hug you without bursting into
flames.

I hurt for you today and again tomorrow
I don't know if I am willing to let you go,
Be free and happy with your own sorrow
While I can't imagine my life glow.

I need to let this pain wash away from me
And be my own lighthouse in the sea
I will be waiting for my futures key
And let you be your own referee.

All I can say, you are my life forever
The two eyes and smile we made
Will carry our spark of lovers
And you will understand why I stayed.

Is that true?

Is that true?
Is it that true we don't end up with
The Love of our life sometimes?
Or there is no love of your life at all?
And you just need to work and communicate
Over and over again
Setting boundaries and compromise
Be there no matter what
And keep your hopes up,
And all you can do is love?

But then they say love is not enough
And life is more than feelings of a heart
Sometimes fighting is exhausting
And sometimes you need to let them go
So they can return
And you can try again and again.

Is that true that to love unconditional
You need to hold the door
While they leaving you with your broken heart?

Is that true that love is more than me and you
And all we can do is have patience?

Is that true that we don't end up with
The love of our life sometimes
And all you can do is let them go?

If this is all true, love is very sad indeed.

I wonder

I wonder if I talk to you one more time
I wonder if I cry one more time
I wonder if I write one more time

Will you see my love and try again?

I wonder if I stayed and didn't leave
I wonder if I loved you till I disappear
I wonder if I kept my pain all to myself

Would you take me back and change?

I wonder if my love was enough
I wonder if I cried too much
I wonder if I was good to you

Would things be differently?

I wonder if we both loved,
I wonder if we both talked and listen
I wonder if we both compromised

Would our happiness make up the cracks?

I can only wonder as the pain I screamed
Destroyed our future and now you can't even be here.

I should

I should have believed you the first time
I should have seen it the first time
I should have ripped you off the first time
I should have locked you out the first time
I should have f ck you the first time
I should have hated you the first time
I should have let you go the first time
I should have not cared the first time
I should have lost you the first time
I should have let you cry the first time
I should have let you make a mistake the first
time
I should have
I should have done it.
I should have but too late now.
Now I am crawling through the mud to get to the
lily water.

If this is love

If this is love
Why does it feel like dying?
If this is love
Why don't you call while crying?
If this is love
Why doesn't it go straight to healing?
If this is love
Why don't you want to come and feel it?
If this is love
Why do I keep wondering what you feeling?
If this is love
Why don't you fight if I am worth it?
If this is love
Why are you offering money
In exchange for peace?

My Theory

And then I met you
And it all made sense
Why I fell in love with you
And why I felt everything so tense.

And then I made you my man
And I saw your worth and flaws
Because I didn't plan
To love and accept no laws.

You know I know what you did
Before you met me
And how you never got the ring
And how you decided to be free.

Your freedom was the price
Of myself digging into abyssal
Of a soul-draining pain and ice
and my loves dramatic fall.

Choose yourself

Letting go is so overdue
Six months past the break
And you still didn't care
And when I say you don't care
I mean, you never called, you never lost your
shit.

You think your ego needs protection
You choose to watch
While the demons were taking me away
Your protected your peace
At the cost of my piece.

I will never understand a man
Who never get in touch with his emotions
But I know you gonna go
Live and get another girl
And there will be 2 ways to hurt me back again.

First, you gonna work and get them out
You will share your fear and flaws
Or you will make the same mistake twice
Till you will understand it wasn't me.

It was me you didn't want
While there was nothing wrong with me
And my nights will get better
My tears will dwell on you
And I will learn to love but choose myself.

There were days I almost let you win
I wanted this love to kill me
To beat me till I was pink dust
To draught the water from my veins
And never let a man come back.

It's hard to accept he doesn't want me
When you grow up unfixed
Where they refused your validation
And then you go and fall in love
And life makes you take a choice.

Learn to undo the trauma damage
That existed in your head
To fix the light in the tunnels
And let the man go
But this time always choose yourself.

Don't say Okay

I hate when they say
Everything will be okay
How can it ever be okay
When literally everything is going down the
drain.

I hate that you think
I am off better alone
And I don't deserve the closure
When I left to see if you are gonna chase.

I hate to ever know
That you moved too quickly
When every kiss feels like cheating
But sad to know you already opt out a long time
before.

I hate to feel
Like I need more than pain
And I need to learn to breathe
When you don't even think of me.

His theory

He said he wanted a family
And I jumped in the queue
I offered my heart hapilly
To live and fight through.

He said - I am not romantic
And still, flirt his way on the side
It was me too much dramatic
And not his will and pride.

He said - I offered you the things
I never offered anybody
While I was asking for the things
I told him - It doesn't require money.

He said again - I love you
While breaking my heart in two
I begged for him to leave, its due
But he stayed to make sure I don't have a clue.

And then I raised my voice
And I said - I can't do this anymore
I was thinking, he will hear the noise
And will turn to see me on the floor.

In the end, he didn't turn
He didn't chase and never spoke
He left the money on the floor
And said: Good luck, I love you too.

All these months
I was confused
So many people said - just leave
He already is past the break
He already got somebody new
He doesn't think or feel at all for you
Just leave and don't ever return.
But I still need to face him
Because he chose me from the queue
And now I see his beauty and his glare
In my daughter's lovely face.

Selfish

I was selfish
Because I saw the look in your eyes
You weren't happy
But I still didn't let you go.
I was selfish
Because I pushed you to do things
You didn't enjoy it and weren't in
Your nature.
I was selfish
When I asked for romantic
But I knew I wasn't the woman
You gonna do it for.
I was selfish
When I felt like I am holding on
Because I was afraid to live
Without you.
I was selfish
When I screamed hurtful words
And make you almost disappear.
I was selfish
Making my love - your love
Without your consent.
You were selfish
That you didn't set up boundaries

And let me know
It's time to let go.
You were selfish
When you said I love you
But I wasn't the woman to
Receive these words.

First and last

Do you want to hear something sad?

Remember the way I looked at you
The first time I met you

And I will remember forever the way you
looked
at me
The last time you left me.

When they ask

When they ask what I wanted
I want to tell them this
I wanted to be his favorite person
And to never feel like this.

When they ask what went wrong
I want to tell them this
I was talking, screaming, kicking
When he left me so confused.

When they ask why you still fighting
I want to tell them this
It's all because I felt safe
And I thought I can change him.

When they ask what is gonna happen
I want to tell them this
I am so tired of chasing
A dream I can never dream.

I am sorry

I am sorry that I made the house home
But you didn't find peace in it.
I am sorry for my overthinking
That made you push me further away.
I am sorry for ignoring the boundaries
When you asked me to listen over and over
again.

I am sorry for pushing my love into you
Without clear instructions.
I am sorry for my anxiety
That made you choose someone else than me.
I am sorry for the calls and messages
That didn't get to you.

I am sorry for the late response
When you finally talked to me.
I am sorry for the sorrow
I build inside of me.
I am sorry that you needed to fix me
When it wasn't yours to fix.

I am sorry for the tears and desperation
That made you not want to be with me.
I am sorry for the sadness

I invented it when I had everything.
I am sorry for the life we build
That only brings arguments.

I am sorry for the time
That we didn't use for us.
I am so sorry for the rejection
That lasted all my life.
I am sorry that you met me
And now we can't afford to wait.

I am sorry for the spending
When it wasn't mine to spend.
I am sorry for the cars
You spend your money on.
I am sorry for the dedication
Of a love that didn't make.

I am sorry for the body
That got me sick and traumatized.
I am sorry for the nights
We didn't spend together.

I am sorry for everything
That made you think you can't come back.

A man

I loved you and I truly hoped
I can change you
Into a man who gave me
Flowers with no reason,
Who called when out
With his friends,
Who texted 'I miss you
I want you right now'
Who spend my birthday
Making me happy,
Who brings home
My favorite chocolate,
Who knows my drink of choice,
A man who got the ring
And made a big show about it,
A man who tickles me
In my favorite spot,
A man who knows my body,
A man that buys ballons
On my big days,
A man that makes memories
And then shares them
Saying 'Look, this is my girl!'.

But I got to love
A man that I couldn't
Change
And instead, I got the man
Who fixed myself.

Love - go figure.

My last letter to you

I want you to know that you lost me
You lost my love
And you lost it because you are a coward.
You are a coward because you can't face your
feelings,
You didn't want to be vulnerable
You didn't want to get to know why
You didn't know how to ask and listen.
I have loved you like I never did anyone
With you, I was able to actually fight
My demons.
I let you in on some pretty vulnerable moments,
I know, I know - I can't put the whole blame on
you
But I can blame you for this again and again
Your ego refused to say whatever
Do you think of me or not?
I blame you for not doing the right thing
And you only did what your parents raised,
I blame you for saying I love you
But then not give a shit about my tears.
I blame you for that I choose you in the
moments
And then you chose just your friends.

You said money is important
But money never pays for love
You said I am fucking with your head and
feelings
But I never gotten to hear - what else?

I have so many feelings
And they coming out boiling hot
I am mad and then I am screaming.
It is not the fear that I am losing you
It is not.
The fact I will never know
Did you ever want me
And why you didn't ever clear the air?
It's the fact I fought alone for us
And you just flashed the bills.
You went and grow up apart
And said to everyone I am crazy
That I argue every time you home
And that I keep on running
But did you ever say
She is crazy but she loves so fiercely
It makes me afraid to leave her alone?
Did you ever say
She wasn't toxic before I met her,
I just left her confused and all the time alone?
Did you ever say
She was never what I wanted
But she gave me a route to escape?

Did it ever cross your mind
I am hurting
And you should be delicate with me?

Did you ever think - I don't want you
But I grow to love you
Your way.